LeBron James

A Basketball Star Who Cares

Kimberly A. Gatto

Enslow Elementary

an imprint of

E **Enslow Publishers, Inc.**

40 Industrial Road
Box 398
Berkeley Heights, NJ 07922
USA

http://www.enslow.com

Enslow Elementary, an imprint of Enslow Publishers, Inc.

Enslow Elementary® is a registered trademark of Enslow Publishers, Inc.

Library of Congress Cataloging-in-Publication Data

Gatto, Kimberly.
  Lebron James : a basketball star who cares / Kimberly A. Gatto.
      p. cm. — (Sports stars who care)
  Includes bibliographical references and index.
  Summary: "A biography of basketball player LeBron James, highlighting his charitable work"
—Provided by publisher.
  ISBN 978-0-7660-3776-2
  1. James, LeBron—Juvenile literature. 2. Basketball players—United States—Biography
—Juvenile literature. 3. African American basketball players—Biography—Juvenile literature.
4. Generosity—Juvenile literature. I. Title.
  GV884.J36G38 2011
  796.323092—dc22
  [B]

                                        2010014921

122010 Lake Book Manufacturing, Inc., Melrose Park, IL

Paperback ISBN 9781598452310

                        Printed in the United States of America

10 9 8 7 6 5 4 3 2 1

To Our Readers:
We have done our best to make sure all Internet addresses in this book were active and appropriate when
we went to press. However, the author and the publisher have no control over and assume no liability for
the material available on those Internet sites or on other Web sites they may link to. Any comments or
suggestions can be sent by e-mail to comments@enslow.com or to the address on the back cover.

Illustration Credits: Associated Press

Cover Illustration: Associated Press

Introduction

LeBron James is one of the top basketball players today. He is a small forward for the Miami Heat in the National Basketball Association (NBA). But there is nothing "small" about LeBron James. He stands six-feet eight-inches tall and weighs 250 pounds. Fans often call LeBron James by his nickname, "King James." That is because he rules the basketball court!

Small forwards like LeBron James are very versatile. They score a lot of points and grab rebounds. James is one of the top scorers in the NBA. Once he scored 56 points in a single game! James also plays good defense. That keeps the other team from scoring points. Even though he is big, he can run very fast. He can block shots and steal the ball.

LeBron James is also a great team leader. He works well with the other players. Sometimes he helps them score. In basketball that is called an assist. James lets his teammates know that he is there for them. He once said, "Ask me to play. I'll play. Ask me to shoot. I'll shoot. Ask me to pass. I'll pass. Ask me to steal, block out, sacrifice, lead, dominate. ANYTHING."

"If there's one message I want to get to my teammates," added James, "it's that I'll be there for them, do whatever they think I need to do."

LeBron Raymone James was born on December 30, 1984, in Akron, Ohio. LeBron's mom, Gloria, was very young. His dad was not around. Gloria worked very hard to support LeBron. But the family was poor. Sometimes they lived in bad neighborhoods. The

Chapter 1

Early Years

LeBron's mom, Gloria, gives him a hug after a big high school game in February 2003.

family often moved from place to place. Once they moved seven times in a single year.

All of this moving was tough on LeBron. He missed a lot of school. He also felt different from other kids. LeBron found an escape from his troubles by playing sports. He especially liked football and basketball. LeBron was good at both.

In his first six games of Pee Wee football, LeBron scored 19 touchdowns. He was even better at basketball. LeBron made dribbling and shooting the ball look easy. He often pretended he was Michael Jordan of the Chicago Bulls. Jordan was one of the greatest basketball players of all time. LeBron dreamed that one day he would become a pro like Jordan.

Back at home, Gloria James worried about LeBron. She did not want him growing up in a bad place. She wanted him to do well in school. Gloria spoke with LeBron's coach, Frankie Walker. He lived in a nice home with his wife and three kids. Walker's son, Frankie, Jr., was LeBron's age. Walker told Gloria that LeBron could live with

Gloria James shows off pictures of her son LeBron before a big game against Reynolds High School in North Carolina in 2003.

them for awhile. That way Gloria could try to save some money.

Gloria wanted what was best for her son. So LeBron went to live with the Walkers. It was a good situation for everyone. LeBron was treated just like the other kids. He had daily chores and homework. He lived in a safe neighborhood. That year LeBron did not miss any classes. He got good grades in school. He even won a school attendance award.

Coach Walker was like a dad to LeBron during this time. He also helped LeBron with his basketball skills. Walker showed him how to play all positions in the starting five. He also showed LeBron how to shoot with his left hand. LeBron worked hard and learned quickly.

Best of all, LeBron was still able to spend time with his mom. They stayed very close. "My mom and I have always been there for each other," LeBron said. "We had some tough times, but she was always there for me."

As LeBron got older, he was taller than the other kids his age. By junior high, he was six feet tall. This helped him reach the basketball hoop. He could score, rebound, and even dunk the ball. LeBron's coaches were amazed at his talent. So were his friends and teammates.

chapter 2

Young Star

LeBron had a group of close pals: Willie McGee, Sian Cotton, and Dru Joyce. Dru's dad was a high school basketball coach. The friends called themselves the "Fab Four." They all played basketball. When it came time for high school, they wanted to stick together. So they decided to go to the same high school. That school was St. Vincent-St. Mary (SVSM) in Akron.

SVSM's basketball team was called the Fighting Irish. LeBron was a starter. He was also the school's star player. In his first year, LeBron's team won the state championship. They won it again the next year. That season, LeBron was named Ohio's Mr. Basketball. This meant that he was the best player in the state. LeBron was the first sophomore ever to win the award.

By his junior year, LeBron had grown to six feet seven inches. He had also become well known. People came from all over to watch LeBron play. Soon the high school arena was too small for LeBron's many fans. The Fighting Irish had to move their home games to a larger building.

LeBron drives to the basket while playing for Akron St. Vincent-St. Mary's in March 2002.

It seemed that everyone was watching LeBron. NBA scouts came to watch him play. The newspapers wrote articles about him. LeBron's photo appeared on the cover of *SLAM,* a national basketball magazine.

LeBron James also continued to win awards. As a junior, he was named Mr. Basketball for the second time. He

LeBron soars above the hoop during a high school game on January 24, 2003.

was also named Player of the Year by *Parade* magazine.

Soon the basketball world was focused on LeBron. NBA superstar Shaquille O'Neal came to watch one of his games. Kobe Bryant sent LeBron a special pair of sneakers. LeBron also met his idol, Michael Jordan. LeBron later said that meeting Jordan was "an unbelievable experience."

Some people thought that LeBron should leave school and become an NBA player right away. Scouts tried to convince him to turn pro. But LeBron and his mom felt that he should finish school. They believed that education was important. After graduation, he would be free to begin his NBA career. LeBron worked hard and did well in school. His favorite subject was earth science.

By his senior year, LeBron had become a celebrity. People began calling him "King James." TV crews followed him to school. LeBron's photo appeared on the cover of *Sports Illustrated* magazine. He won more awards. LeBron was

LeBron calmly puts up a shot during a high school game against Brookhaven in Columbus, Ohio.

Most Valuable Player (MVP) at many games. The Gatorade company named him National Player of the Year. Some of LeBron's games were even shown on TV.

LeBron had become so famous that the Nike company signed a contract with him. He would appear in advertisements for Nike sneakers. He would even have a pair named for him. The contract would last for seven years. It would pay LeBron $90 million!

At seventeen years old, LeBron no longer had to worry about being poor. "King James" had become a superstar.

In 2003, LeBron graduated from high school. That summer, he entered the NBA draft. LeBron attended the draft with his mom. He was chosen first overall by the Cleveland Cavaliers. The "Cavs" were a struggling team. In the 2002–03 season, they had won only 17

Chapter 3

Pro Player

A young LeBron James practices on the court just before making his professional debut for the Cleveland Cavaliers in October 2003.

games. Fans hoped that LeBron could turn the team around.

That year, LeBron did his best to help the Cavaliers win. In his first game ever, he scored 25 points, 9 assists, and 6 rebounds. He even stole the ball 4 times.

LeBrom slam-dunks the ball in a game from his rookie year in the NBA.

The Cavaliers won 35 games that season. They did not make the playoffs, but they had improved a lot. LeBron was named the NBA's Rookie of the Year. This award is given to the best first-year player. LeBron was the first Cavalier to be Rookie of the Year. He was also the youngest player ever to win the award.

DID YOU KNOW?
LeBron did very well in high school. His favorite subject was Earth Science.

In the summer of 2004, LeBron was chosen to represent the United States in the Olympics. The event was held in Athens, Greece. LeBron played alongside many other NBA superstars, including Allen Iverson, Tim Duncan, and Dwyane Wade. As a rookie, LeBron did not get to play too much. The team lost to Argentina and ended up winning the bronze medal.

James shoots over Ron Artest of the Indiana Pacers in December 2003.

DID YOU KNOW?

LeBron was the youngest player in NBA history to score more than 40 points in a single game.

When the 2004 season began, LeBron showed his superstar status. That season he played more minutes than any other NBA player. He became the youngest player to record a triple-double. He also played in his first All-Star Game. The Cavs did not make the playoffs, but won 42 games that season. They were getting closer to becoming a championship team.

The 2005–06 season was a great one for LeBron James. He played in his second All-Star Game. James scored 29 points as he led the East to a 122–120 win over the West. He became the youngest player ever to be named All-Star MVP.

Chapter 4

Star Power

LeBron James tries to dribble around a defending player.

That season, James averaged 31.4 points, 7 rebounds, and 6.6 assists per game. He scored 35 or more points in nine games in a row. Only two other players (Michael Jordan and Kobe Bryant) since 1970 had done that. James also became the youngest NBA player to average 30 or more points per game.

James finished second in MVP voting behind Steve Nash of the Phoenix Suns. *The Sporting News,* a magazine, named James and Nash "co-MVPs." Thanks to James, the Cavaliers now had a winning record of 50–32. They were headed for the playoffs.

The Cavs entered the first round of the playoffs against the Washington Wizards. The Cavs won the series in six games. James averaged 35.7 points per game. The Cavaliers then faced the Detroit Pistons. The Pistons were a very strong team. James played well, but the Cavs lost in seven games. James became determined to do better the next year.

LeBron James puts up a shot over Carlos Delfino of the Detroit Pistons during the 2007 playoffs.

In the 2006–07 season, James took part in his third All-Star Game. That season the Cavaliers tied their record of 50 wins. LeBron averaged 27.3 points per game. The Cavs moved on to the playoffs for the second straight year. In the opening round, they swept the Washington Wizards. It was the first playoff sweep in Cavaliers history.

After beating the Wizards, the Cavs faced the New Jersey Nets. James took his job seriously.

James tries to work around a double-team during a game from the 2007 playoff series between the Cavs and the Pistons.

He led the team, averaging 25 points per game. The Cavs won the series, 4–2. For the first time in fifteen years, the Cavaliers were headed for the Eastern Conference Finals. There, the two best teams in the East would play against each other.

The Cavaliers began the series with two losses to the Detroit Pistons. But James did not give up. He brought the team back to win the next four games. Game 5 was especially exciting. The game was tied after four quarters. It went into overtime. Then it went to a second overtime. James scored with two seconds left in double overtime. The Cavs won the game. James scored 48 points overall, setting another Cavs record. Sports commentators praised James. Marv Albert said that James had "one of the greatest moments in postseason history." Steve Kerr, a former teammate of Michael Jordan, compared James to Jordan.

LeBron James and the Cavs were headed to the NBA Finals.

In 2007, James and the Cavs played in the NBA Finals. It was a dream come true for James. The Cavs were playing the San Antonio Spurs. The Spurs, led by Tim Duncan, were a tough team to beat. James averaged over 25 points per game. But it was not enough. The Spurs swept the Cavs in

Chapter 5

MVP

four games. James vowed to do better the next year.

James continued to play well in the 2007–08 season. He played in his fourth NBA All-Star Game and was again named All-Star MVP. In a game on February 27, 2008, he became the youngest player to reach 10,000 points.

James led the Cavs to a 45–37 record that season. The Cavs once again headed to the playoffs. They faced the Wizards, beating them in the first round. The Cavs then faced the Boston Celtics, who would go on to win the series in seven games. In the final game, James and Celtic Paul Pierce each scored more than 40 points.

That summer, James once again played on the U.S. Olympic team. The Games were held in Beijing, China. James's teammates included Kobe Bryant, Chris Paul, and Dwight Howard. James was no longer a rookie. This time he was a starter and a co-captain. With James's help, Team USA won the gold medal. James was very proud. He told reporters, "It's the biggest thing for me ever. I got

LeBron James goes up for a monster jam while playing for Team USA during the 2008 Olympics in Beijing, China.

to the NBA Finals, and I thought it was pretty big for me. But winning an NBA championship never would compare to winning a gold medal for my country."

In the 2008–09 season, James would continue his winning ways. He became the fourth NBA player ever to lead a team in scoring, rebounds, and assists in one

LeBron James proudly displays the MVP trophy that he earned for his play for the 2008–09 season.

season. The Cavs ended the regular season with a record of 66–16. It was the best record in the NBA that year. At the end of the season, LeBron James was named MVP.

That year the Cavs again headed to the playoffs. In round one, James and the Cavs swept the Detroit Pistons. They swept the Atlanta Hawks in the second round. The Cavs then moved on to the Eastern Conference Finals. It was a tough series. The Cavs lost to the Orlando Magic in six games. James was disappointed, but he set his sights on the next year.

James led the Cavs to a 61–21 record in 2009–10, taking home his second MVP Award. But James was banged up, and Cleveland struggled in the playoffs. In the semifinal round, Boston defeated the Cavs in six games.

After the 2009–10 season, LeBron James left Cleveland. James enjoyed playing with the Cavs, but he needed a change. His friend Chris Bosh had just signed with the Miami Heat to play with their friend Dwyane Wade. James thought they

Chris Bosh, Dwyane Wade, and LeBron James (left to right) pose for the cameras during a welcome party put on by the Miami Heat on July 9, 2010.

would work well together. So he decided to take his talents to Florida.

James looks forward to winning his first NBA Finals in Miami. With James's talent and winning attitude, that is very possible. As James said recently, "Hard work pays off and dreams do come true."

On the basketball court, LeBron James is a fierce competitor. He loves to win. But he knows that there are more important things in life than winning.

Before James became a star, he made a promise to himself. If he ever got rich and famous, he would give back to

Chapter 6

Making a Difference

others. James remembered how it felt to be poor. He wanted to help others in need, especially kids. He later said, "I think the reason why I'm the person who I am today is because I went through those tough times when I was younger."

DID YOU KNOW?
LeBron eats and writes with his left hand, but shoots with his right.

During 2004, James and his mom started a new charity. It is called the LeBron James Family Foundation. This group helps kids in many ways. It also helps single parents. James told reporters, "I told myself if I ever made it to the level I want to be at, I'm gonna give back."

Thanksgiving is a special holiday for James. He is thankful for all that he has been given. Each Thanksgiving, James serves turkey dinners to needy families. In 2009 he served dinners to more than eight hundred people! James said, "It's kind of overwhelming. I'm in a position where I'm able to do things like this. It's not like I have to, it's because I want to. I know I can't fulfill every kid's dream. But I'm thankful I can do something like this."

The LeBron James Family Foundation does a lot of good work. It builds new, safe playgrounds in cities. James often gives kids new bikes to help

LeBron James gives out Thanksgiving turkeys at Antioch Baptist Church in Cleveland in 2005.

them stay fit. Each summer, he hosts a bikeathon to raise money for needy kids. It is called the King for Kids Bikeathon. The event is held in James's hometown of Akron, Ohio. James actually rides his own bike in the event. Other NBA players, like Chris Paul of the New Orleans Hornets, also take part. James said, "It's great to see the smiles on kids' faces. That's the most important thing to me. It really means a lot to them and it's special for me."

Off the court, LeBron James is known as a fun and upbeat person. When not playing basketball, James enjoys listening to music and watching the New York Yankees baseball team. One of his favorite foods is cereal. He especially likes Fruity Pebbles, Frosted Flakes, and Cinnamon Toast Crunch.

James also spends a lot of time with his own family. He remains close to his mom, Gloria. And James enjoys being a dad. His firstborn son, LeBron, Jr., arrived in 2004. James's younger son,

LeBron James is ready to ride just before the start of the King for Kids Bikeathon put on by his LeBron James Family Foundation on August 7, 2010, in his hometown of Akron, Ohio.

Bryce Maximus, arrived in 2007. The boys are already learning to play basketball!

LeBron James is known for being a great basketball player. But his heart is what makes him a champion. He knows that kids look up to him and that he should always do the right thing. LeBron James said, "I have no problem being a role model. I love it. I have kids looking up to me and hopefully I inspire these kids to do good things."

NBA

SEASON	TEAM	GP	FG%	REB	AST	STL	BLK	PTS	AVG
2003–2004	Cleveland	79	.417	432	465	130	58	1,654	20.9
2004–2005	Cleveland	80	.472	588	577	177	52	2,175	27.2
2005–2006	Cleveland	79	.480	556	522	123	66	2,478	31.4
2006–2007	Cleveland	78	.476	526	470	125	55	2,132	27.3
2007–2008	Cleveland	75	.484	592	539	138	81	2,250	30.0
2008–2009	Cleveland	81	.489	613	587	137	93	2,304	28.4
2009–2010	Cleveland	76	.503	554	651	125	77	2,258	29.7
TOTALS		548	.479	3,861	3,811	955	482	15,251	27.8

GP=Games Played
FG%=Field Goal Percentage
REB=Rebounds
AST=Assists
STL=Steals

BLK=Blocks
PTS=Points
AVG=Points Per Game

Where to Write

LeBron James
c/o Miami Heat
601 Biscayne Blvd.
Miami, FL 33132
USA

All-Star Game—A game with the best players in the league as voted on by fans.

assist—The act of passing the ball to a teammate so that he can score.

defense—The act of stopping the other team from scoring.

draft—A lottery in which a team can choose a player.

Most Valuable Player—The most important player on a team.

rebound—The act of taking possession of the ball after a shot.

sophomore—A person in his or her second year in high school or college.

sweep—To win straight games against another team.

triple-double—In basketball, when a player has double-digit stats in three categories.

versatile—The ability to do a lot of different things well.

winning record—When a team has more wins than losses in a season.

Read More

Books

Christopher, Matt. *On the Court With . . . LeBron James*. New York: Little, Brown Books for Young Readers, 2008.

Jacobs, L. R. *Lebron James: King of the Court.* New York: Grosset & Dunlap, 2009.

Sandler, Michael. *Lebron James: I Love Challenges!* New York: Bearport Pub. Co., 2009.

Internet Addresses

Official NBA Site
http://www.nba.com/playerfile/lebron_james/index.html

LeBron James Official Site
http://www.lebronjames.com/

Index